AF430913

The Art of Swimming

MAVEN BOOKS

The Art of Swimming

Richard F. Nelligan

Instructor of Gymnastics, Athletics and Aquatics in Amherst

College Massachusetts

MAVEN BOOKS

Chennai   Trichy   New Delhi

This edition has been published in india by arrangement with Carson Books, UK

ISBN 978-93-90877-17-1 **Maven Books**

All rights reserved   No. 44, Nallathambi Street,
Printed and bound in India   Triplicane, Chennai 600 005

MJP 1007   © Publishers, 2021

Publisher's Note

The legacy of a country is in its varied cultural heritage, historical literature, developments in the field of economy and science. The top nations in the world are competing in the field of science, economy and literature. This vast legacy has to be conserved and documented so that it can be bestowed to the future generation. The knowledge of this legacy is slowly getting perished in the present generation due to lack of documentation.

Keeping this in mind, the concern with retrospective acquiring of rare books has been accented recently by the burgeoning reprint industry. Maven Books is gratified to retrieve the rare collections with a view to bring back those books that were landmarks in their time.

In this effort, a series of rare books would be republished under the banner, "Maven Books". The books in the reprint series have been carefully selected for their contemporary usefulness as well as their historical importance within the intellectual. We reconstruct the book with slight enhancements made for better presentation, without affecting the contents of the original edition.

Most of the works selected for republishing covers a huge range of subjects, from history to anthropology. We believe this reprint edition will be a service to the numerous researchers and practitioners active in this fascinating field. We allow readers to experience the wonder of peering into a scholarly work of the highest order and seminal significance.

MAVEN BOOKS

CONTENTS

Life Saving Instructions, pages 36, 62 and 65

PART III—Diving and Somersaults

PART IV

PART V

PART VI

ILLUSTRATIONS

INTRODUCTION

RECENT investigations by some of the leading educators of our time have brought to light the deplorable fact that about twenty-five per cent of the students in our men's colleges are unable to swim a stroke, that many others have a very imperfect knowledge of the art and could be absolutely of no use to others in distress and danger of drowning. If such are the facts regarding a class so favored as this, what must be the conditions in our secondary schools, and among the youth of our land generally? How large a proportion of our young women must there be who are unable to swim a stroke? It is to be hoped that in the near future our educational institutions generally will give the subject attention, and make swimming and the knowledge of life-saving methods a part of the curriculum.

The United States Government, recognizing the absolute necessity of a thorough knowledge of swimming in time of war, not only for the crossing of rivers, cutting of cables, etc., but also as the best means for securing physical development and strength, places the art in a high position in the requirements at the army and navy academies at West Point and Annapolis. No single exercise or game will produce such wonderfully good results in health, strength and power as swimming, if correct methods be employed.

The humane societies of the world have already done much to educate the public in methods of life-saving by their publications and medals, and the certificates offered for proficiency in the art. They might, however, go still further by adopting some universal test—given at set places and times each year—which would be the means of drawing together men and women from all parts of the world to compete for their certificate.

The time is well spent in those forms of athletics which bring honor to the club, the school, or the college, as football, baseball, and track contests. But it is also desirable that young men acquire a practical knowledge of some exercises that both contribute to their own physical welfare in youth and also may prove to be especially useful in later life. Among them swimming deserves first place, owing to the fact that it may be the means, not only of self-preservation, but also of saving the lives of others. To stimulate a livelier interest in this most valuable of all forms of exercises, and to give some assistance to the acquirement of it, the author presents this little volume.

PUBLISHER'S NOTE

The writer of this book has for many years studied and taught all the various strokes used in the water. He is an expert at both long and short distance racing and is familiar with methods of life saving, which he has successfully used on several occasions. The book is carefully written so as to appeal to experts, but it considers also the novice. It is seldom that one individual combines to such a marked degree as does Mr. Nelligan the practical knowledge of swimming with the ability to express it. He differs from several leading exponents of swimming in his description of the strokes, but only after careful study and trial of their mechanics.

The grades which are proposed in the latter part of the book, in Part VI., are an innovation in aquatics and deserve careful consideration. Already this subject has attracted the attention of school and college authorities as being a ready and practical method of increasing knowledge of swimming. Amherst College was the first to adopt it and others are likely to do so as soon as practicable. We will be pleased to correspond and assist as we can those who may desire further information than is contained in this book.

With the increased interest which has arisen in this most useful and beneficial sport, the book will doubtless be most welcome to swimmers and to instructors.

PART I

ESSENTIALS

1. Swimming Drill on Land.

The following drill will be found very useful in teaching beginners the proper movements of the arms and legs for the first strokes in swimming, and can be taught in the schoolroom, in the gymnasium and at the side of the bath.

A. ARM EXERCISES.

a. Position: On the command "Position," bend the arms at the elbows until the hands are in front of the chest, thumbs about six inches apart, and push the hands forward and upward with the palms turned downward, and the head bent slightly backward.

b. Ready:

One: On *one*, turn the palms slightly outward and sweep the arms around in a quarter circle until they are at right angles with the body.

Two: On *two*, bend the elbows until the hands are again in front of the chest with the palms downward.

Three: On *three,* shoot the hands forward as in a. Position and sweep the arms around as in Exercise One.

Four: Halt. Lower the arms and stand attention.

NOTE.—Each exercise should be repeated sixteen times and at about the rate of sixteen to the minute.

B. LEG EXERCISES.

a. Position: On the command "Position" place the hands on the hips.

b. Ready:

One: On *one* bend the left knee, turning it outward, the left heel touching the inside of the right knee, and the toes pointing downward.

Two: On *two,* straighten the left leg backward and downward until the great toe touches the ground at the left.

Three: On *three,* draw the left foot to the right.

Four: Halt. On the command, "Halt," stand at attention.

NOTE.—Each exercise should be repeated until proficiency is attained, first with the left leg and then with the right, after which the movements should be executed alternately.

C. COMBINED ARM AND LEG MOVEMENTS:

a. Position: On the command "Position," shoot the arms forward as in Exercise One.

b. Ready:

One: On *one,* sweep the arms around as in Exercise Two; at the same time raise the left knee as in exercise One of the leg drill.

Two: On *two,* close the elbows to the sides as in Exercise Three, and at the same time lower the left leg as in Exercise Two of the leg drill.

Three: On *three,* shoot the hands forward as in Exercise One, and at the same time draw the left foot to the right.

Four: Halt. Lower hands and stand at attention.

NOTE.—When proficient with the arms and left leg, the right leg should be brought into play; after which the legs should be used alternately.

2. Swimming Drill in the Water.

After attaining proficiency in the Land Drill the pupils may line up and count off by twos before entering the water. Having entered the water, at the command, "Support," let the odd numbers place their right hands under the chins of the even numbers. On the command, Ready, let the even numbers submerge all but the head. On the word, "Go," let the even numbers endeavor to swim to the opposite side of the pool, while the odd numbers walk along beside them, supporting their heads above the water. At the command, "Change Ranks," let the even numbers furnish the support, while the odd numbers in turn try to swim back to the starting point.

A. THE BREAST STROKE.

The breast stroke is the key to swimming of all kinds. It should be the first taught to beginners, because it is the easiest to acquire, since its movements are more natural than any of the others. When this is thoroughly mastered, various other strokes can be easily learned. The highest authorities on physical culture agree in thinking that for all around physical development and the production of a well set-up carriage of the human body no movements known can equal the breast stroke. The effort of keeping the head above the surface strengthens the neck muscles; thus making it easy to hold the head erect, the chest is forced forward in breasting the waves, the arms and legs are strengthened by being used alternately to propel the body, and the swimmer is forced to breathe deeply and regularly against the strong resistance of the water. If the breathing is not in unison with the leg and

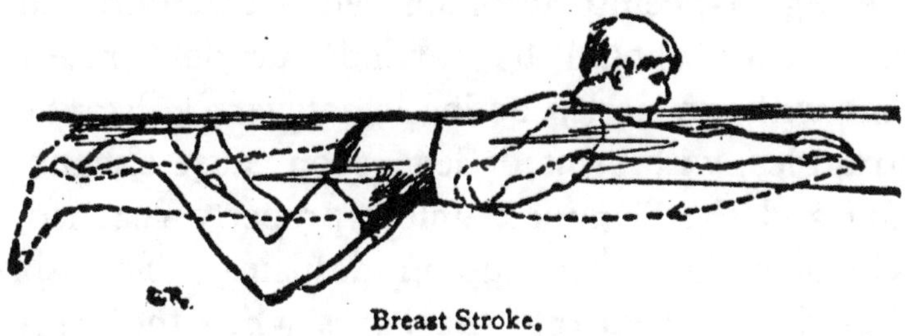

Breast Stroke.

arm movements, and the lungs not well inflated with each stroke, the swimmer soon tires, while it becomes impossible to make fast time over a long course.

The following description will give an idea of the manner in which the breast stroke should be performed. In starting the swimmer lies flat on his breast with the legs straight and together, the arms being extended in front of the head and about four inches beneath the surface. The palms are now turned outward and the straight arms are drawn through the water and carried well back like a pair of oars in rowing. When the arm stroke is nearly finished, the knees are turned outward and drawn slowly about half way up to the body. The legs, with the knees still separated, are then straightened diagonally back-ward with a kick, and brought together sharply like the closing of a shears. As the legs are are thrust outward and backward the arms are shot forward with the palms downward, and re-main stationary in this position, in order to keep the head above the surface, while the closing of the legs is being accomplished. The different movements should be carried out deliberately and with no jerky action whatever. Frantic struggles, with arms or legs, soon cause exhaustion and the beginner, unless properly coached, will sometimes give up in despair. The air should be drawn into the lungs when the arms are ~~thrust~~ forward, and expelled as they ~~approach the sides of the body.~~

B. To Learn Without a Teacher.

While the foregoing description relates to a perfect performance of the breast stroke when under the eye of a competent instructor who will insist upon accuracy in detail and also give reasons for the theory which he applies, yet good instruction is not possible in all cases and the enthusiastic beginner is thrown upon his own resources. Even under such conditions, it is possible to learn the breast stroke well enough to enable one to reach shore from a considerable distance.

Having carefully selected a place free from currents and weeds where the water is clear and the bottom sloping gradually, the learner should enter and wade out until the water reaches to the waist. He should then take a deep breath, bend the legs until the head is beneath the surface and open the eyes. After looking around and at the bottom for a few seconds, the operation should be repeated until the head can be placed under water with full confidence.

The next step will teach the novice the fact that it is possible to lie in the water close to the surface for some little time without sinking.

After facing the shore, a full breath should be taken, the body inclined slowly forward and the arms extended in front and near the surface. Next the feet should be raised from the bottom and with the eyes open the body should be straightened out near the surface. It will be found that while in this position if no attempt is made to raise the head out of the water the body will float for a considerable time. Should the head be raised the feet will sink.

After some practice at floating in this position the next step should be to bring the arms, with the palms turned ~~upward~~ OUTWARD backward to the sides as in the regular breast stroke. If the eyes are gazing at the bottom it will be seen that, even with no movement of the legs, the body will move toward the shore. When the shore can be approached in this manner, the legs should be brought into play as in the ordinary breast stroke when, if the eyes are still open, an appreciable gain in speed will be noticed.

A few days careful practice of this method will enable the enthusiast to reach the shore with the head slightly raised above the water, after which progress in the regular breast stroke should be found easy. The writer wishes to repeat that great care should be exercised in selecting a place free from currents and weeds, as otherwise after the feet are removed from the bottom there is danger of being carried into deep water; and it is also wise to have a friend at hand in case of an emergency.

A summary of the above method is as follows: *First,*—Wade out waist deep, bend the legs until the head is under water, with the eyes open. *Second,*— Lie on the surface face down and float. *Third,*—Use the arms to reach shore. *Fourth,*—Use arms and legs in reaching shore. *Fifth,*—Endeavor to reach shore with the head slightly raised.

Only after considerable practice in shallow water should the swimmer venture beyond his depth, and even then it is a wise precaution to have a boat or a good swimmer at hand, for the reason that in many instances swimmers have

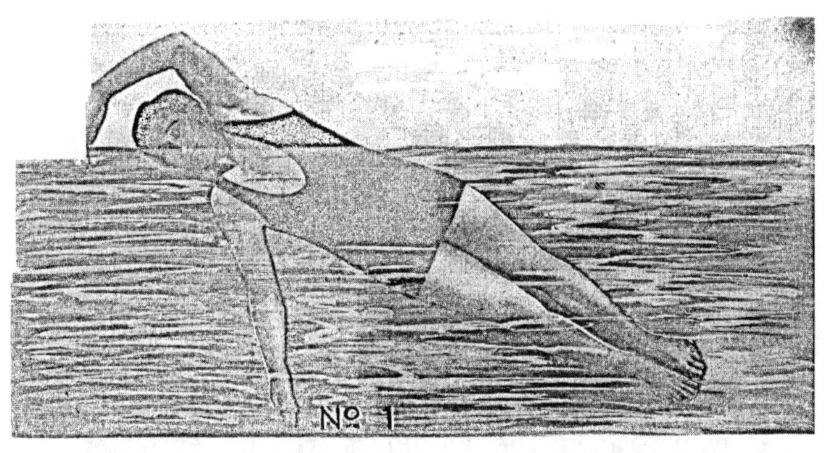

OVER-ARM SIDE STROKE. (See page 19)

been known to lose confidence, and forget their best laid plans and even the directions of competent teachers, when venturing into deep water for the first time.

By the above method the writer learned the rudiments of the breast stroke well enough to swim five miles and others have done much better. The main points to keep in mind are, that all movements must be executed slowly and deliberately, the head should be raised no higher than is necessary for breathing purposes, and it is well to keep the shoulders well under water..

While the breast stroke is useful and even absolutely necessary for beginners in the art, still it is no longer considered by experts as being of much use for speed, when compared with more modern methods. It is, however, a remarkable fact that all of Captain Webb's long distance swims were accomplished with this stroke, and it is related that he accomplished his marvelous swim across the English Channel in this manner. It is only reasonable to suppose that had he been proficient in the more modern methods of natation his performance would have been even more astonishing.

C. Side Strokes.

Of all strokes known to swimmers, the most generally useful is the Over-Arm Side Stroke. This stroke, although difficult to acquire, when once mastered enables the swimmer to cover long distances rapidly and with less exertion than is required in any other method. The movements should be practiced while lying upon the left as well as upon the right side; thus enabling the swimmer, when tired, to rest somewhat, by a change from one side to the other. The best exponents of the modern side stroke are J. Nuttall, champion of the world; J. McCusker, the

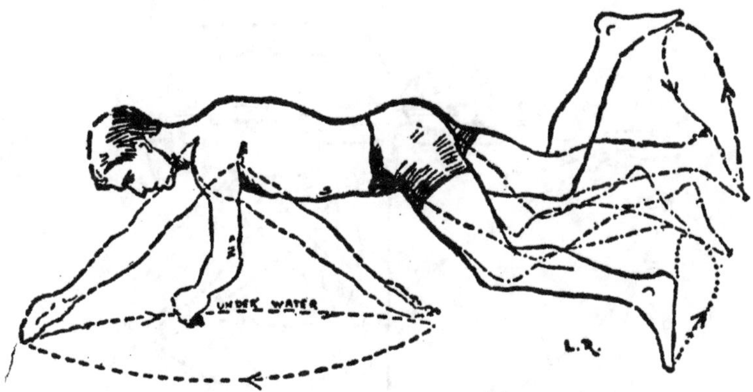

Over-Arm Side Stroke, No. 1, showing left arm and both legs.

former champion of America, and Cavill, the Australian champion. In a three-mile race, held at Newport, in 1904, which was won by Nuttall, all three men used the over-arm side stroke from start to finish. The most expert sidestroke swimmers usually swim upon the right side so that the heart action may not be impeded.

For a description of this stroke we will assume that the swimmer is lying upon the right side. At the start the right arm is extended rapidly forward, and then drawn downward towards the right thigh without any bending at the elbow. The hand should be flat and the fingers closed. When the hand is within about a foot of the thigh, the elbow is bent in the form of a right angle, the palm is turned so that the thumb is nearest the body, and the arm is again shot forward for another stroke. The left arm, slightly bent, is carried forward above the surface as the

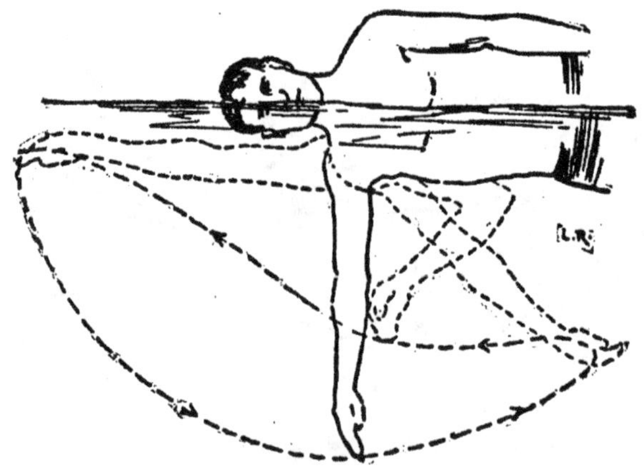

Over-Arm Side Stroke, No. 2, showing right arm.

right arm is being pulled through, and just as the right arm moves forward for the next stroke, the left arm enters the water about a foot in front of the face, and is drawn towards the left hip. The left arm stroke should not be made too long, as the greatest power is applied when the arm, above the elbow, is at a right angle with the body. As the left hand reaches a point opposite the shoulder, the left knee is drawn slowly up in the same manner as in climbing stairs, while at the same time the right foot is drawn backward just as it is when about to kick a foot-ball.   As the left hand is about to leave the water for the next stroke, the left knee is straigh-tened with a jerk and the legs immediately brought together with a snap, the heel of the left foot meeting the instep of the right foot.

It will be readily seen that the leg propelling power is furnished mostly by the back of the left leg and the instep of the right foot. The legs remain straight with the feet extended while the right arm is drawn through the water.

From the above description of this complex stroke it is evident that there are three distinct movements merging one into the other; viz. right arm, left arm and legs in one, two, three, order.   When performed in this manner, the body moves along steadily without pausing be-tween strokes.

KICK AT TIME ARM IS PULLED THROUGH WATER.

Some swimmers execute the kick at the same time that the left arm is pulled through the water; but careful experiments have proven that this method, while good, is inferior to the other.

A common fault in this, as in nearly all strokes, is to draw up the knees too far when preparing for the flip of the legs, thus wasting strength by nullifying the effect of the kick and causing the body to stop between strokes, instead of moving steadily forward. When we consider the fact that in order to swim a mile it is necessary to make a very great number of strokes, it becomes evident that in order to make fast time there should be no perceptible pause between strokes. The swimmer who by careful study and practice succeeds in making continuous progress, other things being equal, will always win the race. The fastest swimmers separate the feet not much further than they do in brisk walking. This forward movement should be performed slowly, while the kick should be executed vigorously like the flip of a pickerel's tail. It is a mistake in side swimming to spread the legs to the sides as in the breast stroke; for it causes the body to turn on the breast, and thus impedes progress by presenting a large surface to the water. From start to finish the body should remain on the side with the head half under water, excepting, of course, in a rough sea, when the head is raised partly for the sake of vision and partly to prevent the waves from covering it. Beginners should take advantage of every opportunity of seeing expert side-stroke swimmers in the water, since more can be learned by watching an expert swim the length of a tank than by reading and amount of detailed description.

INDEPENDENT ACTION OF ARMS AND LEGS.

Since writing the preceding description, the following variations of the Over-Arm Side Stroke have proven to the author faster for a short distance than the methods already described; and future experiments may show that even for distances over a mile it is, for the majority, the stroke par excellence.

In the one, two, three order of arms and legs, as described, it will be noticed that the legs remain straight while the right arm is drawn through the water; consequently the legs are doing nothing in the meantime to propel the body. Therefore it occurred to the writer that instead of allowing the legs to be idle part of the time they should, if possible, be used to force the body forward, if greater speed was to be obtained; hence the experiment. Having completed the kick and closing of the legs, they were instantly drawn up and the movement repeated.

It will be readily seen that this method calls for an independent action of legs and arms, and all parts of the body are continually in action. The writer's conclusion is, that, as the arms and legs differ in size, length and strength, they should be used independently. For the best results this method calls for that perfect muscular co-ordination which is so noticeably lacking in many individuals whose physical training has been neglected during the period of adolescence.

Many swimmers, without competent instruction, find it next to impossible to master the Over-Arm Side Stroke in any form, for the simple reason that, as the upper arm is carried forward in preparation for the propelling backward movement, sufficient downward pressure with the lower arm is not exerted and consequently the head sinks and the natural breathing is so much interfered with, that the swimmer becomes discouraged and is more than likely to revert to the breast stroke. If after faithful practice it is found impossible to acquire the over-arm side stroke the swimmer may try the Under-Arm Side Stroke which, though not as speedy a method as the over-arm is nevertheless found, by most swimmers, to be superior to the breast stroke.

UNDER-ARM SIDE STROKE.

Having completed the downward and backward movement of the upper arm, in unison with the kick and closing of the legs, it is thrust forward for the next stroke beneath, instead of above, the surface of the water. The lower arm is used as in the over-arm side stroke. The disadvantage of reaching forward under water, in preparation for the positive part of the upper arm stroke, instead of above the surface as in the over-arm style, becomes obvious when we consider the fact that in the former method the resistance is greater than in the latter.

SIDE-STROKE WITH CRAWL MOVEMENT OF THE FEET.—The writer is now experimenting with the following variation of the side-stroke which gives promise of great speed. The arms are used as in the ordinary over-arm side stroke. The legs are spread in preparation for the kick, until the feet are about eighteen inches apart. Having completed the closing of the legs with a snap, they are not allowed to remain still while the right arm is executing the pull, but instead, the top leg continues slowly to the rear and the under leg slowly to the front, bending the knees slightly until the feet are about nine inches apart. From this position the feet are again snapped together, the propulsion coming from the instep of the upper foot and from the sole of the lower foot. This latter movement is then reversed, the upper foot passing to the front and the lower foot to the rear. This final movement of the stroke should be finished with the feet together and immediately the legs should be drawn up for the next stroke. The whole movement of the legs should be timed so as not to interfere with the regular movement of the arms. Careful observation will show that the second leg movement is similar to the leg and foot movement in the Crawl Stroke described later.

Up to the present time, all writers on the swimming art have placed too much value on drawing the knees well up to the body in the negative part of all strokes excepting the Crawl. They have evidently overlooked the fact that if one were passing rapidly through the water, and wished to stop suddenly, one of the best ways of doing so would be to draw the thighs towards the body and spread the legs as far apart as possible. Drawing the legs up vigorously has the same effect upon the body in swimming that reaching forward for a stroke with a pair of oars without feathering has in rowing, providing, of course, the blades were kept under water. The legs cannot be feathered through the water on the recovery, as the hands can be in the breast and under-arm side strokes, hence the necessity of a comparatively slow and not too wide leg movement.

As the conformation of the individual may have much to do with the selection of the best form of side-stroke, it will be well for the enthusiast to give each variation of the side-stroke a careful trial over different distances under the watch. This will prove interesting to the swimmer and will lead to valuable discussion among the members of swimming clubs.

SUMMARY.

A summary of the above methods of side stroke swimming is as follows:

First—Right arm, left arm and legs in one, two, three order.

Second—Kick at the same time that the left arm is pulled through.

Third—Independent action of arms and legs.

Fourth—Under-arm side-stroke.

Fifth—Side-stroke and crawl movement of the feet.

d. The Trudgen Stroke.

For distances in open water over one hundred yards, and up to about five hundred yards, no single stroke known at present can equal the

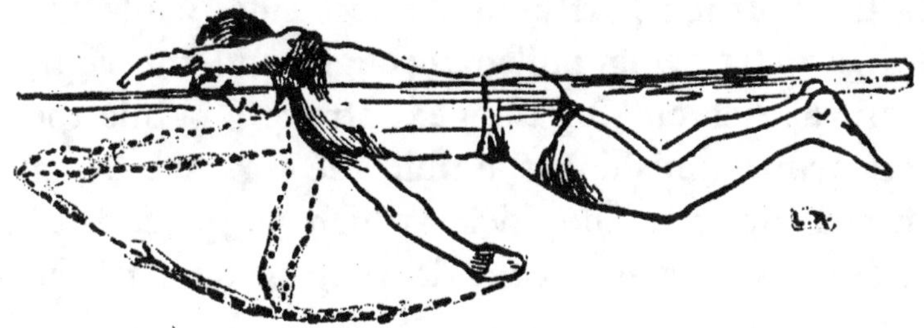

Trudgen Stroke, No. 1, showing right arm.

famous "Trudgen" introduced into England in 1873, by J. Trudgen. He learned it from the natives of South America, and by means of it won many championships in his time.

In the Trudgen stroke, when well performed, the body rolls from side to side, while the arms are thrust forward alternately above the surface, and then drawn downwards and backwards until the hand nearly touches the leg, when it is

again thrust forward for another stroke. When
the right arm is beneath the surface, the body is
turned well over on the right side, and while in
this position the left arm is carried forward
through the air for another stroke. The body

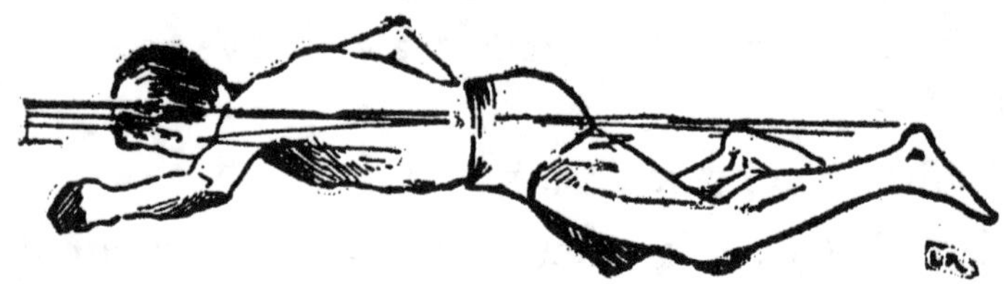

Trudgen Stroke, No. 2, showing left arm (right arm just being
drawn out of water).

is then turned partly on the left side, while the
left arm is being pulled through, and the right
arm reaches out for the next stroke. While the
left arm is finishing the pull, the legs are being
drawn up for the kick, which is performed
slightly in advance of the drawing through of the
other arm.

Modifications of the Trudgen are in vogue

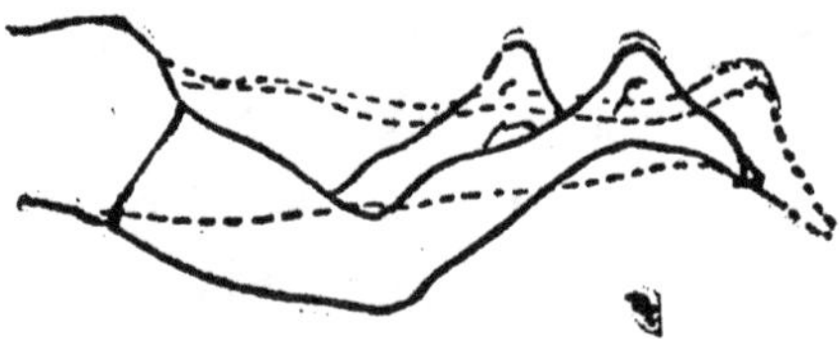

Trudgen Stroke, No. 3.   Half top view showing leg movement.

among the inhabitants of the Hawaiian Islands,
the Indian tribes of South America, and the life-
guards at our summer resorts. A thrust with

the legs combined with each arm movement is sometimes used; but it is doubtful if any advantage is gained by this method, as the extra kick is very exhausting. When swimming to a person in danger of drowning, the swimmer should never do this, but preserve his strength or two lives may be lost. Swimmers of exceptional endurance have been known to cover distances over 440 yards and up to one mile, using the Trudgen. This is especially valuable for life saving purposes over short distances.

e. THE CRAWL STROKE.

The stroke which produces the greatest speed over a short distance is known as the "Crawl"

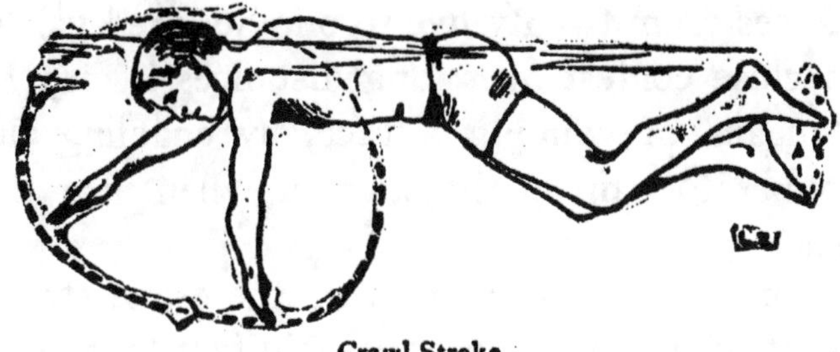

Crawl Stroke.

and has been introduced into the United States from Australia within a year or two.

In this stroke the swimmer lies flat in the water with his face submerged, and the leg propelling power is furnished principally by short alternate upward and downward movements of the feet, without any spreading of the legs, the ankles and knees serving as the hinges. The extreme range of these upward and downward movements of the feet is about eighteen inches. The arms are carried forward alternately above the surface and backward through the water like the paddles of a side-wheel steamer.

For long distance swimming this stroke is almost useless, as it is very exhausting, owing principally to the fact that the breath must be held, excepting at intervals when the head is raised forward or at one side for breathing purposes. In addition the swimmer finds it difficult to keep a straight course. In tank swimming where guiding lines are painted on the bottom, the crawl stroke in any of its many forms is undoubtedly the best, when striving for speed over distances from twenty-five to one hundred yards. In a close contest over long distances it may be the means of winning a race, by enabling the swimmer to gain at the start or when near the finish.

At present no two men swim the crawl stroke exactly alike, but it is a noticeable fact that those who have succeeeded in mastering it in some form have reduced their previous records many seconds, and hence it is reasonable to conclude that in some form, which time and experimental study alone shall determine, it is the fastest of all known swimming strokes. The description of the stroke as here given may have to be varied by individuals according to size and build. The advocates of the crawl stroke have already proven beyond doubt that the ~~scissors~~ kick as performed in the breast stroke is no longer of any use whatever for racing purposes.   The reason for this is that as the legs are drawn up and spread to the sides, preparatory to the kick and closing of the legs, the body stops between strokes and the swimmer soon tires from the increased leg action.

Richard Cavill of Australia and Handy of Chicago can swim faster without the use of the legs than with them, and many Trudgen swimmers can do the same.   On the other hand it is a noticeable fact that the upward and downward movement of the feet in the crawl, will propel the body forward without any movement of the arms.   Hence we must conclude that a proper leg and arm motion combined will produce the greater speed.

The following variations are noticeable among exponents of the crawl stroke:

A double over-arm stroke is combined with a wide up and down leg movement.   The legs are timed so as to alternate with the opposite arm.

A short and rapid paddle-wheel motion of the arms is combined with a very fast upward and downward "fluttering" of the feet.

A ~~long~~ Trudgen arm stroke combined with a slow pedalling motion of the feet, and a quarter turn of the body from side to side.

Daniels, the present amateur champion at all distances up to one mile, said recently, "I have come to the conclusion that a double overarm stroke, with moderate reach, and an up and down continuous, alternate motion of the legs from the knee, give the best results."

In the A. A. U. four hundred and forty yards championship contest held in the New York Athletic Club pool on Feb. 23, 1906, Daniels, using the crawl stroke for one hundred yards, was closely pressed by Schwartz of the Missouri Athletic Club. He then gradually drew away, and at about two hundred yards changed from the crawl stroke to something new in swimming, viz. a combination of the crawl and Trudgen strokes. Having completed the kick in the Trudgen, Daniels did not allow his legs to remain idle the fractional part of a second, as is done by most Trudgen swimmers. Instead he performed upward and downward alternate movements with the feet, as in the crawl stroke, before separating the feet for the next Trugden stroke. This extra upward and downward movement must have helped him greatly as he won the race by about twenty-five yards in the American record time of five minutes, fifty and two-fifths seconds. In the crawl stroke Daniels rolls considerably from side to side and the arms and legs are used independently. His Trugden kick, in the combination stroke, is performed while upon the right side; and his forward reach is longer than that of most crawl stroke swimmers. There is an appearance of ease and grace in his work rarely seen in sprint swimming; and this, no doubt, helps to make him pre-eminent in longer distances.

f.   To Swim on the Back with Legs Only.

This is a very useful exercise and should be well practiced by those wishing to qualify as life savers; for the reason that the most popular

Swimming on Back, with Legs only.

method of towing a person, is to swim upon the back with the hands placed beneath the arm-pits, although some swimmers prefer placing the hands at the sides of the head of the drowning person. (See Life-saving section.) The swimmer turns on the back, folds the arms upon the chest, and with the legs executes the same movements used in the breast stroke. Many fast swimmers use the legs in much the same way as they are used in the over-arm side stroke. This is a very useful exercise and valuable, as is shown under Life-saving section.

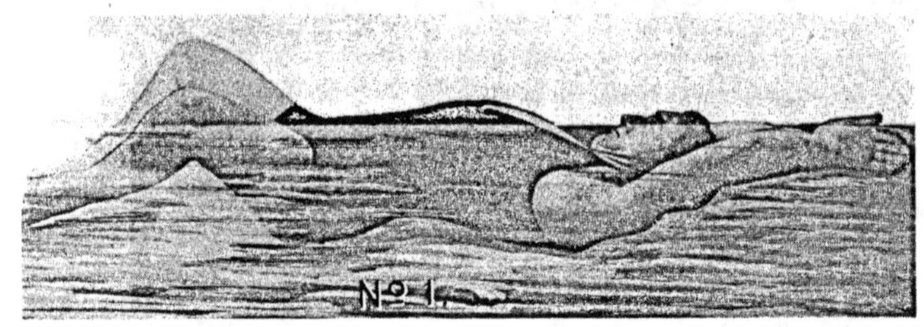

Swimming on Back, with Legs and Arms.   (See page 33.)

g. SWIMMING ON THE BACK WITH ARMS AND LEGS.

In this stroke the movements of the legs should be the same as in the preceding exercise. As the legs are drawn up for the kick, the arms are stretched out beyond the head and beneath the surface with the palms turned upward. The open hands are now turned so that the thumbs are near the surface, when the straight arms are drawn down by the sides like a pair of oars, while at the same time the legs perform the kick. A

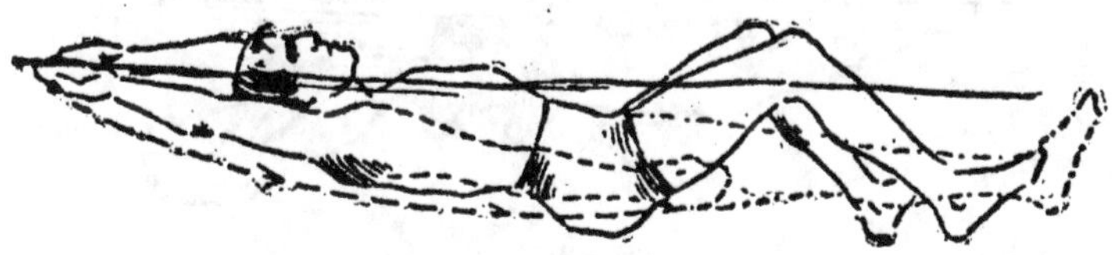

Swimming on Back, with Legs and Arms.

faster method is to pass the arms above the surface in reaching back for the downward sweep of the hands. Some swimmers reach back with the arms alternately.

h. FLOATING.

Floating in fresh, as well as in salt water, is one of the most useful and agreeable of the many accomplishments of the expert swimmer, and can be learned by almost anybody, especially women. It is accomplished by lying on the back, keeping the lungs well inflated, and the arms stretched back of the head, while the knees are drawn up and turned so that the legs will be submerged. Nearly, if not all, books on swimming state that the legs should be straight. While this may accomplish the purpose in salt water, the writer has demonstrated the fact many times that in fresh water, excepting in the case of a very fat person, or one with unusually small legs and large lungs, the legs, unless drawn up, will sink the body. The reason for this is that in the bent position the legs and feet are nearer the

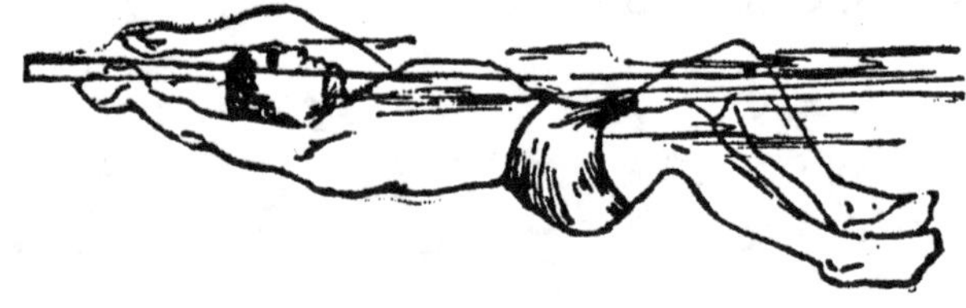

Floating.

lungs, and if at the same time the arms are extended back of the head, the body will be balanced much better than is possible with the legs straight. In rare instances we find persons who cannot possibly float, on account of the small capacity of the lungs, and also at the same time because of the density of the bones and muscles. Still, it is possible for these, by slight movements of the hands, to keep the head up for a long time, even though suffering with cramps.

i. Cramps.

Cramps usually attack the legs first; but the experienced swimmer, with a slight knowledge of bodily mechanics and a cool head, will experience but little difficulty in turning on his back, and alternately resting and stretching the offending limb or limbs until the trouble has passed away. If the arms are attacked it is a simple matter to stop using them, and yet keep afloat by a proper use of the legs. Even when both the legs and arms are cramped at the same time, it is possible to still keep the head above the surface of the water by floating. The average swimmer when cramped in any part of the body or limbs tries to use the offending part all the more strenuously, thus aggravating the trouble, and, in addition, does all in his power to climb upon the surface. This, of course causes exhaustion and a sinking of the head. He also has a great inclination to open his mouth and call lustily for assistance, without taking any precaution whatever to keep the water from entering the lungs. Should some friend swim to his aid, he is almost sure to attack him if approached too soon and to do all in his power to thwart the good intentions of his would-be-rescuer. A cool head and knowledge of the fact that the specific gravity of the human body, even with the lungs deflated, is but little greater than that of fresh water, would preserve many lives from drowning. The so-called cramp in the stomach is usually, if not always, a pain in the bowels. This pain does not alarm the expert, but, on the other hand, scares the novice until he becomes excited, and makes him struggle until exhausted. After much inquiry among intelligent swimmers and an experience since childhood in all kinds of fresh and salt water swimming, ranging in temperature from fifty to eighty degrees, the writer can find no evidence of a well authenticated case of cramp in the abdominal muscles; and even should it occur, excepting perhaps in very severe form, it seems possible for the expert swimmer to combat it successfully. A wise precaution for the inexpert against the possible attack of cramp is not to go too far from shore unless it becomes necessary.

Proficiency in the following drill will be useful in teaching swimmers how to act when attacked by cramp.

> Class swim breast stroke! Rest right leg!
> Class swim breast stroke! Rest left leg!
> Class swim on back! Rest both legs.
> Class swim on back! Rest both arms!
> Class float!

j. THE RESCUE OF THOSE IN DISTRESS.

The greatest honor that a swimmer can attain is the Humane Society's medal for life saving. Medals in all other branches of human endeavor pale into insignificance when compared with this. It has been rightly called the Victoria Cross of swimming.

In attempting a rescue, if time permits, as much clothing as possible should be removed, though the expert swimmer seldom removes more than the shoes and coat. If the distance is not too great, the Trugden stroke (See page 26) is most frequently used on account of its speed. The rescuer should be extremely careful not to approach near enough to be seized by the one in distress while struggling on the surface. When the drowning person becomes pretty well ex-

Method of Rescue.

hausted, the rescuer should approach from behind, to prevent being clutched, and, placing the hands under the arm-pits of the sinking person, or at the sides of the head, swim upon his back to the nearest landing. If help is near, it is better to simply keep the head of the drowning one above water until assistance arrives. The rescuer should bear in mind that it is not necessary to lift a body above the surface of the water in order to tow it. Such an effort tends to sink the rescuer, and makes his task more exhausting than if he simply keeps the nostrils above water. Another mistake is to bend the arms, thus drawing the rescued too near, which, of course, tends to sink and exhaust him. A very good method is to place the forearm under the chin of the drowning man, or grasp his hair, and swim upon the side.

Far too little attention has been given to practice in life saving. All swimmers should learn how to do this by practice upon one another until proficient.

Should both wrists be seized, the rescuer should press downward, thus causing the attacking person to sink, while the rescuer is buoyed up. The elbows should then be raised outward, and the hands turned inward; the arms should be bent, and a vigorous push with one or both knees or feet against the body will do the rest. Breaking-away movements should be executed with the utmost speed, to prevent the rescuer from being drawn under water. When attacked by a very powerful person, however, from whom it is impossible to break away when near the surface, it is best to take a good breath and go with him below the surface, where, in his excitement, he will soon lose consciousness and fill the lungs with water. The rescuer can then easily escape from his clutches and rise with him to the surface. The so-called "dead man's grip" is a misnomer. A most deadly grip is that in which the rescuer is caught around the neck with the arms, and at the same time around the body with the legs. The expert life saver will rarely, if ever, allow himself to be caught in this manner. However, should he be caught thus, he should take a full breath and, going under water, place one hand over the nostrils and the other upon the shoulder cr behind the back of the person, and force the head quickly backward. If possible, the rescuer should deliver a blow in the face with his head. This may seem cruel, but when clutched the rescuer is justified in using any means in his power to free himself to save the lives of both. In all breaking-away methods the rescuer should first endeavor to pinch the nose so that the other will be forced to open his mouth to breathe, and thus permit the water to enter the lungs. It will then be easy to get free from his grasp. If swimmers in distress would not become excited it would be far easier to effect rescues. They would simply need to place the hands very lightly upon the rescuer's shoulders, and, letting the legs float, allow him to tow them to a place of safety. In effecting a rescue a grave mistake is sometimes made by trying to swim too rapidly. In this way the rescuer becomes exhausted and places both lives in danger.

PART II

EXHIBITION SWIMMING

Exhibition swimming is a never-ending source of enjoyment and usefulness. Apparently there is no limit to the movements which the body may perform in the water, and all swimmers should strive for proficiency in some of them, in order that the body may be under complete control in case of emergency.

1. Front Somersaults.

After a few breast strokes and a full breath, the arms should be stretched out at the sides, knees drawn up, and the body bent forward and the head lowered. While in this position the

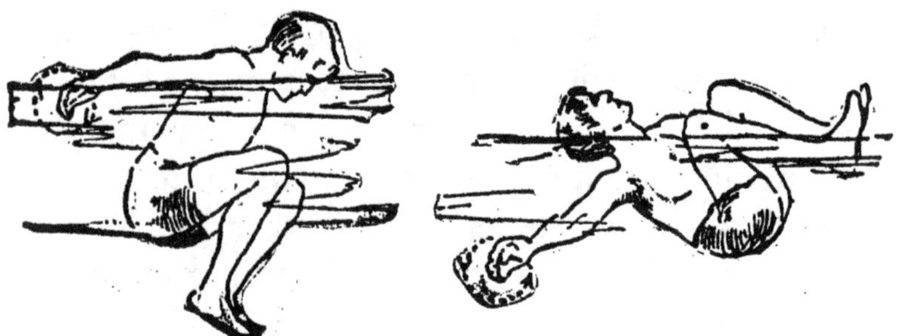

Front Somersault.   Back Somersault.

hands perform sculling motions from front to rear and upward, thus causing the body to turn completely over. The air in the lungs should be changed when the head comes above the surface, thus enabling the swimmer to repeat the exercise at will.

2. Back Somersaults.

After swimming a few strokes on the back, the knees should be drawn up as in the front somersaults, while the head is thrown well back. The arms should be extended at the sides with the palms turned upward and the sculling movement of the front somersault reversed, which will enable the swimmer to turn over backward. The movement should be repeated and the breath changed between somersaults.

3. Over-arm Spiral.

To perform the Over-arm Spiral, the swimmer should start by swimming a few strokes upon the breast. The left arm is now thrust forward

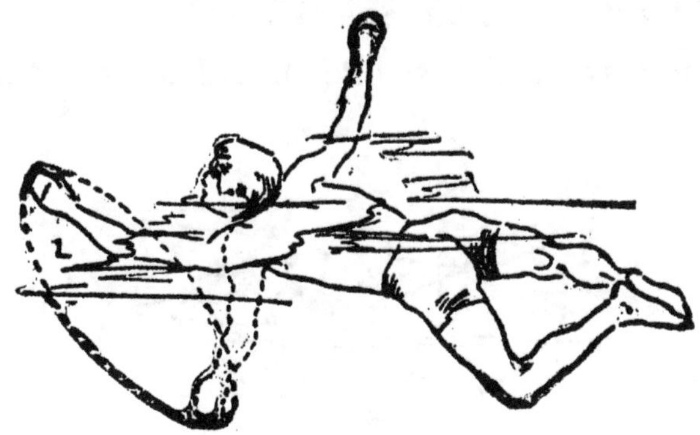

Over-Arm Spiral, No. 1.

above the surface and pulled downward and to the left, at the same time that the kick is performed; this will cause the body to turn on the back. The right arm is now thrown above the head and backward, and is then drawn downward and towards the left thigh, causing the body to turn face downward. In the right arm movement the legs should be straight until the

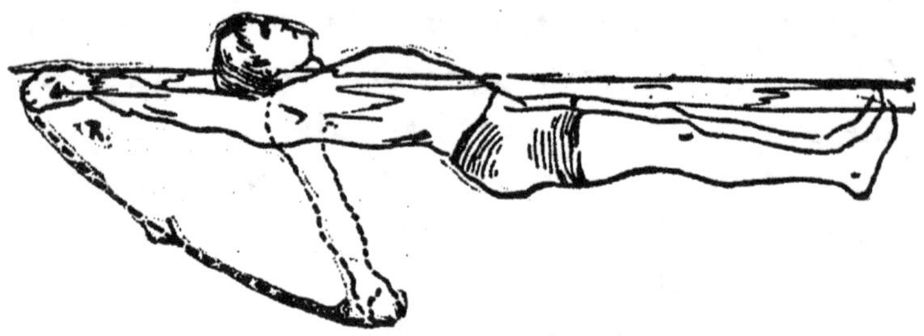

Over-Arm Spiral, No. 2.

pull with the right arm is nearly completed, when they are drawn up for the next stroke. When well performed the spiral is a fairly rapid stroke.

4. Right and Left Spiral Stroke.

The start in this stroke should be the same as

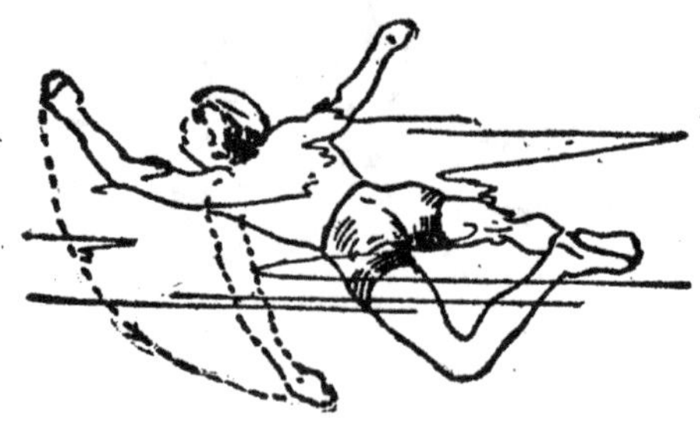

Right and Left Spiral.

in the preceding spiral, but the swimmer should make a complete turn as the left arm is pulled through. The right arm is now thrust forward

above the surface, and then drawn downward
and to the right, causing the body to make a full
turn in the opposite direction. The legs should
execute a kick with each downward movement
of the arms.

5.   Swimming to the Right and Left Sides.

While lying with the breast down, in order
to swim to the right side, the left arm and leg
alternately with the right arm and leg should be
forced from right to left and slightly downward.
The arms should be extended well in front of
the body, and while in the act of returning from
the left to the right side for another stroke, the
palms should be turned down so that the hands
will cut through the water and not impede progress.   In the active part of the stroke, the palms
are turned to the left so that the thumb of the
left hand will be turned downward and that of
the right hand upward. To swim to the left side
the movements are reversed. .

6. Treading Water with Arms above Surface.

This is a somewhat difficult movement, owing,
principally, to the fact that the arms and shoulders should be well above the surface, which, of
course, tends to sink the body. To accomplish
this feat, the swimmer should start from a perpendicular position, maintained by treading
water, that is by alternate upward and downward movements of the arms and legs, the arms

being under water.   The arms should now be raised well above the head while the legs, working principally from the knees, are raised upward and outward and then thrust downward and inward, the feet performing a sort of spiral movement.   When well performed, in muddy water or far from shore, the onlooker is led to believe that the performer is standing on the bottom.   Good judgment should be used as to when and where this trick is performed, as it may be the means of leading novices into deep water.

7.   The Spinning Top.

The swimmer turns upon the back, draws the knees well up to the chin, raises the feet above the surface, and, with sculling motions of the hands from right to left, causes the body to re-

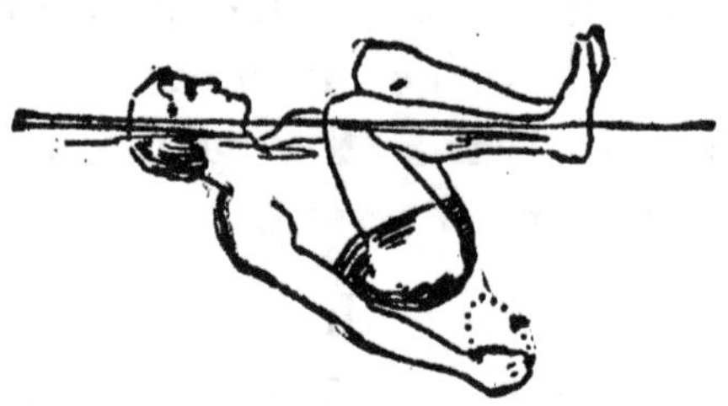

Spinning Top.

volve to the right.   By reversing the movements of the hands, the body will, of course, revolve in the opposite direction.

8.   Sculling on the Back with Head Foremost.

The swimmer takes his position lying on the

back with the legs straight, the toes above the surface, the back hollow and the arms at the sides. He then first carries the hands backward and slightly upward with the palms down, then turns the palms in the direction of the feet and presses vigorously downward and in the direction of the feet, thus causing the body to move along head first. The whole movement should be from the elbows and wrists only, and the circles described by the tips of the fingers not more than six or eight inches in diameter. In this, as

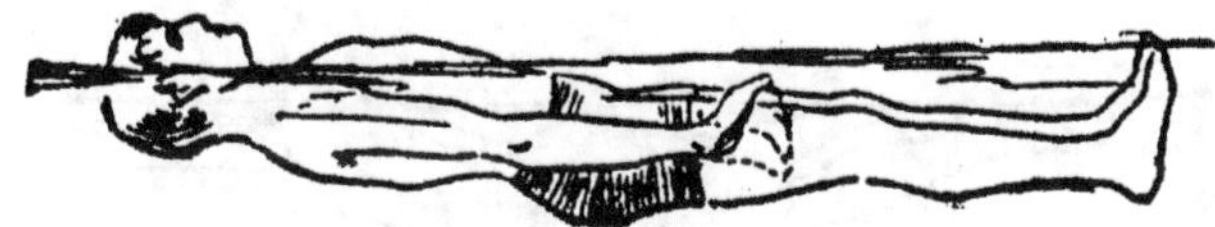

Sculling on Back, head foremost.

in the other sculling exercises, great pressure should be brought to bear on the downward movement of the hands, so as to keep the middle third of the body from sinking. Small movements of the hands heighten the effect of the exercise from a spectacular point of view.

Sculling on Back, feet foremost.

9. Sculling on the Back with Feet Foremost.

To perform this exercise the movements of the hands, as described in the preceding exercise, should be reversed; thus causing the body to move feet foremost.

10. **Sculling on Breast with Head and Feet Foremost.**

Sculling while lying on the breast, both in the direction of the head, as well as in the direction of the feet, is rather more difficult than when lying upon the back. In both movements the back should be hollow, the head drawn well back, while the heels are slightly above the surface.

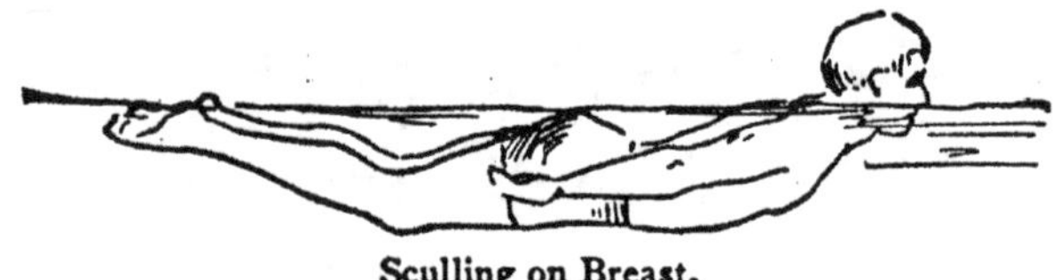
Sculling on Breast.

The movements of the arms in both exercises are much the same as those necessary in order to make progress while sculling on the back. Sculling is an excellent exercise for strengthening the arms and producing an erect carriage of the body.

11. **Porpoise Swimming.**

To imitate a porpoise the swimmer takes a full breath, and, after swimming a few strokes under water, suddenly rises, head first, above the surface by a vigorous kick and a backward and downward movement of the arms. When the head rises above the surface the arms should be held at the sides, while the legs remain straight. The head should now be inclined downward, the stomach drawn in and the back rounded, and if the stroke has been made with sufficient vigor, the back and finally the legs will appear and dis-

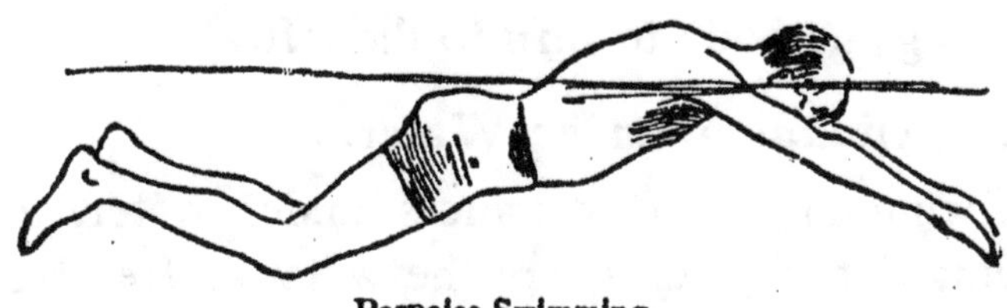

Porpoise Swimming.

appear, to be followed by another stroke and a reappearance of the porpoise. The breath should be changed when the head is above the water.

12. The Steamboat.

The swimmer turns upon his back, and, while sculling head first, the feet are drawn alternately up to the thighs, as in the action of walking upstairs; the feet are then kicked vigorously backward, the soles of the feet being the main source of propulsion. The leg movement should be very rapid so as to agitate the water as much as possible. A downward pressure of the palms will keep the head up.

13. Log-Rolling Right and Left.

The swimmer turns on his back, the hands being at the sides and open, the legs straight and the whole body quite rigid; then, by an almost imperceptible turn of the head and body to the right side, aided by a downward pressure of the left hand and an upward pressure of the right, the body will turn over to the right side. A number of turns should be made to the right side, after which the movements should be reversed, causing the body to turn to the left.

14. Swimming under Water.

Swimming short distances under water, and diving for objects where the water is free from weeds is an excellent practice, and may be the means of saving life in cases where the body sinks before the rescuer arrives. Care should, however be taken not to remain under until nearly exhausted, for by so doing grave injury may be done to the lungs. Attempts to swim great distances under the water should be discouraged by all teachers of swimming.

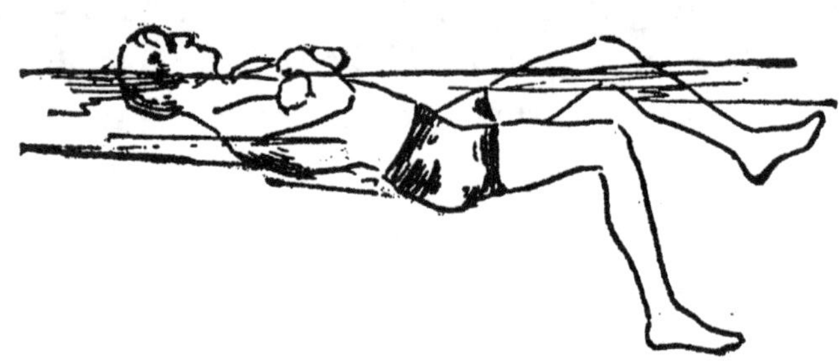

Marching on the Water.

15. Marching on the Water.

The swimmer lies on the back, and, with the arms folded or pressed against the sides, pro-

BREAKING AWAY FROM A DROWNING PERSON. (See page 38.)

gresses feet foremost, by alternate movements of the legs, as in walking. The pressure should be applied in the backward movement of the legs, and the forward movement should be done gently.

16. Undressing in the Water.

To be able to undress in the water may at some time in the swimmer's life be useful, and it is well to practice it occasionally. The usual method is to remove first the coat, second the vest, third the shoes—by breaking the shoe-strings if possible—fourth the trousers and so on. While practising, a friend should be near to render assistance should the swimmer become entangled in his clothing.

PART III

DIVING AND SOMERSAULTS

NOTE.—These exercises, for their best performance, require a spring board but may be done from the bank of river or lake, or from other elevation above the water.

1. **Running Header.**

After a short run the swimmer springs from both feet, inclines the body forward and enters the water head first.

2. **Front Jacknife.**

This dive differs from the running header in that the spring is made so as to launch the body upward in an almost perpendicular position. When at the highest point the abdomen is drawn in, the body bent forward and the diver enters the water as in the running header, but nearer the starting point.

3. **Back Jacknife.**

The diver stands at the end of the springboard, with the heels projecting well over the end. After a spring backward, the body should be bent as in the front jackknife dive, thus causing the swimmer to enter the water head first.

4. **Backward Dive.**

The swimmer stands as in the back jackknife

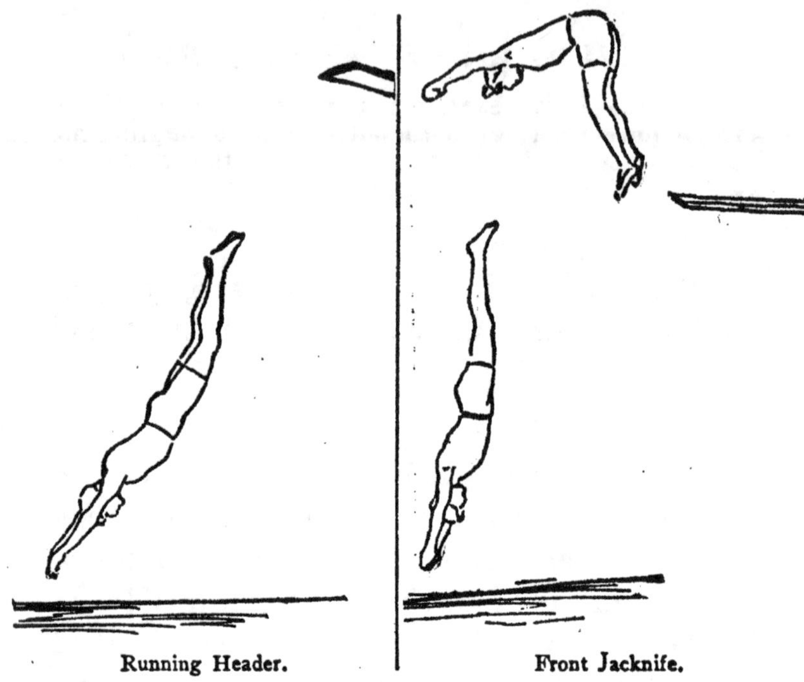

dive, and, with a light spring backward, throws the arms above the head. In the descent the back is toward the spring board and the body plunges in head first.

5. Twisting Back Dive.

The start should be the same as in the backward dive, but as the feet leave the springboard the body is turned to the left or right and enters the water as in the running header.

6. Side Dive.

The swimmer stands at the end of the board, with the left side toward the water, the left arm

Back Jacknife.

Backward Dive.

is raised above the head, a spring is made and the water is entered sideways. The dive should also be made on the right side.

7. Back Somersault from Spring-board.

The heels should be well over the end of the board, in order that the spring may be made from the toes; the body should be inclined backward to avoid striking the board as the body turns over.

8. Twisting Back Somersault.

The start is the same as in the back somersault,

Twisting Back Dive.   Back Somersault from Spring-board

but as the feet leave the board the head is turned sharply to the right or left, causing the body as it turns over to twist in such a way as to enter the water feet first with the back turned toward the spring board.

9. Front Somersault from Spring-board.

A short run, a quick spring, a doubling up of the body, with the head thrown forward, will turn the body over so that the swimmer will enter the water feet first.

Twisting Back Somersault. | One and One-Half Somersaults.

10. One and one-half Somersaults.

After turning over once, as in the front somersault, the body should remain doubled up until another half turn is made, and the water entered head first.

NOTE.—A diving competition may be conducted on the basis of one hundred points for a perfect performance in all ten exercises, and it will always prove interesting and amusing to performers and spectators.

Front Somersault from Springboard.

PART IV

SWIMMING EXERCISES FOR DEVELOP-MENT OF WEAK PARTS OF THE BODY

For the development of weak and undersized parts of the body the following swimming exercises, described in this book, will be found useful.

1. To deepen the chest and straighten the shoulders, swim the breast stroke with little or no leg action. (See page 12.)
2. To broaden the chest and develop the front chest muscles, swim the Trugden stroke without the aid of the legs. (See page 26.)
3. To develop the muscles under and back of the shoulders, swim on the back, using the arms only. (See page 33.)
4. To strengthen the waist muscles, use the spiral strokes. (See pages 41-42.)
5. To make strong a weak back, scull on the breast. (See page 46.)
6. To develop the back of the thighs, use marching on the water. (See page 48.)
7. To develop the abdominal muscles, practice the spinning top. (See page 44.)
8. To develop the muscles of the forearm and hand, practice the different sculling movements. (See pages 45-46.)
9. For all-round development, use the Trudgen breast and over-arm side strokes. (See pages 17-26.)

TRAINING FOR CONTESTS

The diet should be generous and varied, and consist of such food as experience has shown to be best suited to the individual case. No hard and fast rule is necessary and any ordinary table will furnish all that is required. For two or three weeks before beginning active practice in the water, assuming of course that the swimmer has no organic defect, it is well to take vigorous walks of from three to five miles across country, the distance to be governed by the natural strength of the individual. An occasional slow run of from three hundred to eight hundred yards will also be found beneficial in the way of improving the breathing powers. Having returned from the cross-country exercises, a turn at the chest weights for five or ten minutes will strengthen the arms and chest muscles. In the absence of chest weights the same time may be profitably employed in using dumb bells weighing from three to five pounds. Care should be taken not to take vigorous exercise of any kind until about two hours have elapsed after a full meal. All exercise should be followed by a vigorous rub-down with coarse towels. Where an attendant is available, the body should be thoroughly massaged from head to foot to keep the muscles in a flexible condition. This preliminary course of training will strengthen not only the swimming muscles proper, but also the heart; and make the more vigorous work in the water easier and more pleasurable than it otherwise would be. Having taken the preliminary course of exercise on land, the swimmer should now indulge in long, slow swims once a day, for a week or two, of from four hundred to eight hundred and eighty yards, finishing with a burst of speed of about twenty-five or fifty yards. This will develop endurance and speed. After the swim no time should be wasted before the rub-down and dressing in order to avoid catching cold. After this preliminary work on land and water, the average amateur swimmer can keep in good condition by swimming two or three hundred yards daily for endurance, and then after a rest and rub down, a swimming sprint of from thirty to fifty yards may be taken for the purpose of developing speed. The swimmer should be timed in every practice swim, that he may know how he is getting along, and set a pace which he can maintain from start to finish. A competent friend should watch for faults in style that they may be corrected without loss of time, and a smooth, easy movement be developed. This amount of swimming should prepare a man for a race of one hundred yards. Occasionally the full distance should be covered at racing speed, but the main sprint work should be over distances somewhat shorter than the distance to be covered in the race. For distances over one hundred yards and under one half mile, the training should be somewhat different; longer and faster swims are necessary in order to develop greater endurance. A certain amount of speed swimming should be taken, for the reason that many a race is won by a good sprint at the finish. In training for distances up to four hundred and forty yards, about three hundred yards should be covered daily at nearly racing speed. For distances over four hundred and forty yards the work is harder. The speed should be worked up gradually until about three-quarters of the distance can be covered rapidly. About once a week double the distance should be covered at about three-quarter speed, and once a week a time trial may be taken. Before commencing work in the water, swimmers who are inclined to leanness, should endeavor to take on weight. In most cases, where the digestive apparatus is in good condition, the weight can be increased by a generous indulgence in the fat-making foods, such as eggs, milk, certain kinds of fish, sweets, milk chocolate, etc.

Swimmers should remember that, while immersed, a good coating of adipose tissue tends to keep the body warm, makes it more buoyant; and enables one to cover long distances without becoming cramped. In the absence of a competent instructor and coach, the aspirant for swimming honors should be extremely careful lest he overdo, and in consequence suffer from that enemy to all athletic success, viz., staleness. Because one man gets into good condition by following a certain system is no proof that a like system will prove equally good in all cases, owing to the differences in constitutions and habits.

At times during the training period the swimmer loses heart in his work; the time trials are unsatisfactory, peevishness comes on, and frequently there is a loss of weight ,appetite and sleep. This condition is known as staleness, and, in most cases, is the result of too long, too fast or too frequent swims before the body has been prepared by a preliminary course of light training, such as is recommended in the preceding section. In the absence of a competent trainer the best remedy for stalness is a complete rest from swimming, change of air and a very nourishing diet. For a complete recovery of form it is sometimes necessary to rest from three to six days; and in severe cases a longer rest is often required.

PART V

THE MASSACHUSETTS HUMANE SO-CIETY'S TEST AND CERTIFICATE

a. CERTIFICATE.

The Humane Society of the Commonwealth of Massachusetts has consented to award its Certificate of Proficiency in Swimming and Life Saving—a copy of which is given herewith—to the students of Amherst College under the following conditions. The certificate will be given to that student who, in June of each year, for a test made under the supervision of the Department of Hygiene and Physical Education of the college makes the best record in the following test:

b. TEST.

1. Swim the Breast Stroke—100 yards.
2. Swim the Trudgen stroke—50 yards.
3. Swim the Over-arm Side stroke—150 yards.
4. Swim on the Back—25 yards.
5. The Cramp Drill (see page 34.)
6. Rescuing the Dummy.*

*The dummy will be represented by an old suit weighted and sunk at the deep end of the swimming pool. The swimmer will dive, swim the length of the pool, bring the dummy to the surface and swim with it to the starting point.

7. Demonstration of the Massachusetts Humane Society's method for restoring persons apparently drowned.

This award will mark an advance step, both for the Humane society and the college in stimulating swimming and life saving. It would seem to the writer desirable for other educational institutions to apply for similar recognition as an incentive to their students to attain proficiency in this most valuable accomplishment.

The Massachusetts Humane Society has also given permission to print the following instructions for saving drowning persons, their rules for restoring the apparently dead; and also the use of their plates for illustrations.

Instructions for Saving Drowning Persons by Swimming to Their Relief.

1. When you approach a person drowning in the water, assure him in a loud and firm voice that he is safe.

2. Before jumping in to save him divest yourself as far and as quickly as possible of all clothes; tear them off if necessary; but if there is not time, loose, at all events, the foot of your drawers, if they are fastened, as, if you do not do so, they will fill with water and drag you.

3. On swimming to a person in the sea, if he is struggling, do not seize him then, but keep off for a few seconds till he gets quiet, for it is sheer madness to take hold of a man when he

is struggling in the water, and, if you do, you run a great risk.

4. Then get close to him and get fast hold of the hair of his head, turn him as quickly as possible upon his back; give him a sudden pull and this will cause him to float; then throw yourself on your back also and swim for the shore; both hands having hold of his hair, you on your back and he also on his, and, of course, his back to your stomach. In this way you will get sooner and safer ashore than by any other means, and you can easily thus swim with two or three persons; the writer has even, as an experiment, done it with four, and gone with them forty or fifty yards in the sea. One great advantage of this method is that it enables you to keep your head up, and also to hold the person's head up you are trying to save. It is of primary importance that you take fast hold of the hair and throw both the person and yourself on your backs. After many experiments it is usually found preferable to all other methods. You can in this manner float nearly as long as you please, or until a boat or other help can be obtained.

5. It is believed there is no such thing as a death grasp; at least it is very unusual to witness it. As soon as a drowning man begins to get feeble and to lose his recollection, he gradually slackens his hold until he quits it altogether. No

apprehension need, therefore, be felt on that head when attempting to rescue a drowning person.

6.   After a person has sunk to the bottom, if the water be smooth, the exact position where the body lies may be known by the air bubbles which will occasionally rise to the surface, allowance being, of course, made for the motion of the water, if in a tideway or stream, which will have carried the bubbles out of a perpendicular course in rising to the surface. A body may often be regained from the bottom before too late for recovery by diving for it in the direction indicated by these bubbles.

7.   On rescuing a person by diving to the bottom the hair of the head should be seized by one hand only, and the other used, in conjunction with the feet, in raising yourself and the drowning person to the surface.

8.   If in the sea it may sometimes be a great error to try to get to land. If there be a strong "outsetting" tide, and you are swimming either by yourself or having hold of a person who cannot swim, then get on your back and float until help comes. Many a man exhausts himself by stemming the billows for the shore on a back-going tide, and sinks in the effort, when, if he had floated, a boat or other aid might have been obtained.

9.   These instructions apply alike to all circumstances, whether as regards the roughest sea or smoothest water.

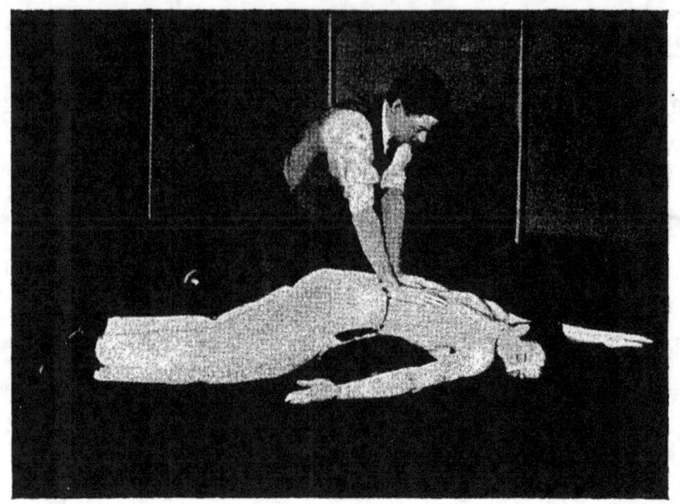

Fig. 1.   Removing Water from Stomach and Lungs.   (See page 65.)

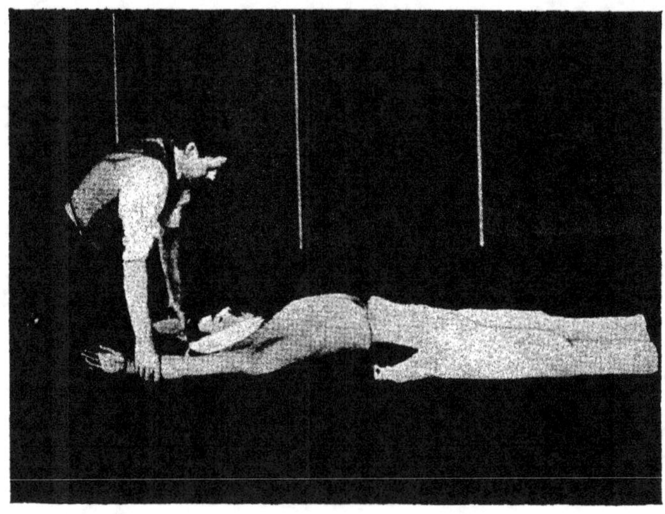

Fig. 2.   Inducing Inspiration.   (See page 66.)

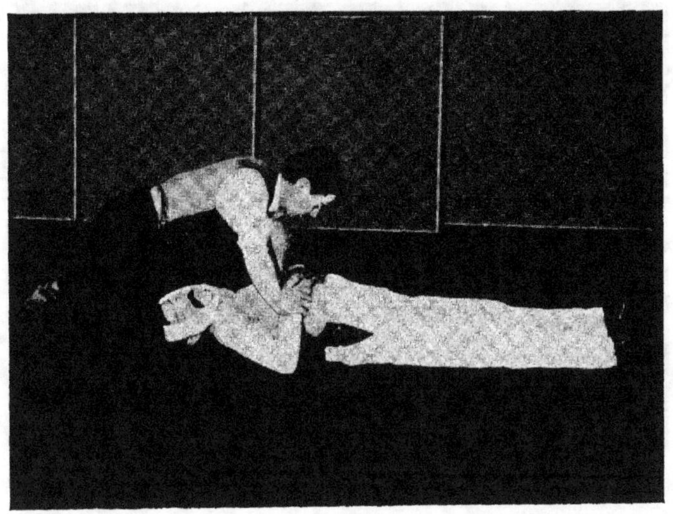

Fig 3. Producing Expiration. (See page 66.)

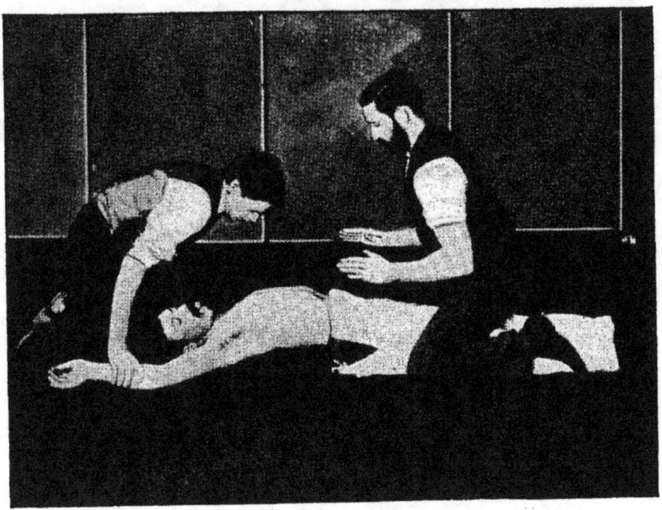

Fig. 4. Inducing Inspiration (with two operators)   (See page 66)

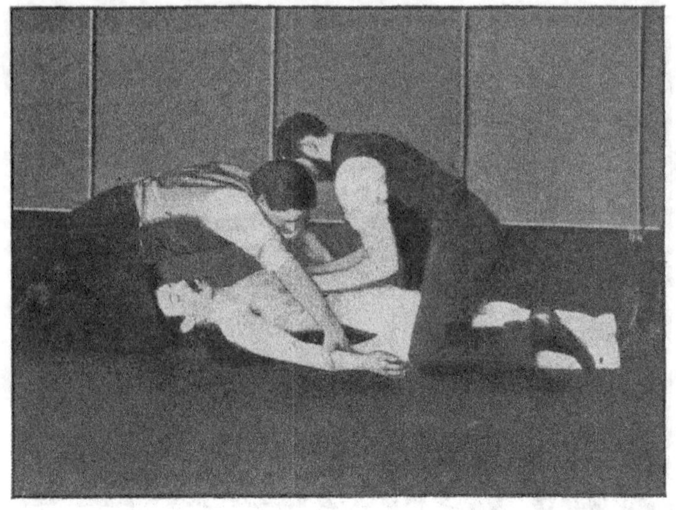

Fig. 5. Producing Expiration (with two operators). (See page 66)

Massachusetts Humane Society Medal for Saving Life (obverse)

Instructions for Restoring Persons Apparently Dead from Drowning.

Rule 1. Unless in extreme cold weather, when there may be danger of freezing, do not move the patient, but instantly expose the face to a current of cold air, wipe dry the mouth and nostrils, rip the clothing so as to expose the chest and waist, and give two or three quick smarting slaps on the stomach and chest with the open hand. If the patient does not revive, proceed at once as follows:—

Rule 2. To draw off the Water from the Stomach and Lungs.—Turn the patient on his face, place a large roll of clothing beneath the stomach and press heavily on the back and spine over it for half a minute, or so long as fluids flow freely from the mouth. (Fig 1.)

Rule 3. To Produce Respiration.—If no assistance is at hand and you must work alone, place the patient on his back with the shoulders slightly raised on a folded article of clothing. Draw forward the tongue and keep it projecting beyond the lips. If the lower jaw be raised, the teeth may be made to hold the tongue in place; it may be necessary to retain the tongue by tying a handerkerchief under the chin and over the head. Grasp the arms just below the elbows, and draw them steadily upwards until they nearly meet above the head. (This enlarges the capacity of the chest and induces inspiration.) (Fig. 2.) Next, lower the arms to the side, and press firmly downward and inward and backward on the sides and front of the chest, over lower ribs and sternum. (This produces expiration.) (Fig. 3.)

Repeat these measures deliberately and perseveringly twelve to fifteen times in every minute. Occasionally rub the limbs upward from the extremities toward the heart, and dash cold water in the face.

Rule 4. If an assistant is at hand, and two can work together, have one kneel at the patient's head and one astride the hips of the patient, facing the patient's face. (Fig. 4.) Proceed as given above, save that when the operator at the head lowers the arms to the sides the second operator presses on the sides and front of the chest backwards and downwards, throwing all his weight into it. (Fig. 5.) The method followed by two workers is the same as that by one, save that the second operator applies the pressure on the chest, and in the time when the arms are being raised applies friction and warmth to the body.

Rule 5. Send for medical aid, stimulants and warm blankets and clothes as soon as possible.

Rule 6. Keep up the efforts for fully **two** hours, or until the patient breathes.

Rule 7. Practise drying and rubbing from the beginning in so far as possible without interfering with the movements of artificial respiration.

Rule 8. After-Treatment.—As soon as the breathing is established, let the patient be stripped of all wet clothing, wrapped in blankets only, put to bed comfortably warm, but with a free circulation of fresh air, and left to perfect rest. Internally, give a little brandy or hot water or other stimulant at hand every ten or fifteen minutes for the first hour, and as often as necessary.

PART VI

METHOD OF GRADING COMPETITIVE SWIMMING

With the fresh impulse which has been given swimming of late, especially competitive swimming, there has arisen a demand for some method of grading the competitors. This has been responded to first at Amherst College by the adoption of the following swimming regulations:

1. **Swimming Regulations at Amherst College.**

In June of each year all members of the Sophomore class, excepting such as may be excused by the physicians of the college, will be required to pass a satisfactory examination in the following exercises:

a. The Breast Stroke, 100 yards,
b. The Over-arm Side Stroke 150 yards,
c. The Trudgen Stroke, 50 yards,
f. Swimming on the Back with Arms and Legs, 25 yards,

Honor or Advanced Classes.

After passing the swimming requirements of the college, such students as desire, may seek membership in the first, second and third Honor

Classes. Membership in the first requires a successful examination in

1. Front Somersaults in the Water.
2. Back Somersaults in the Water.
3. Over-arm Spiral.
4. Right and Left Spiral Strokes.

Membership in the second requires a successful examination in

5. Swimming to the Right and Left Sides.
6. Treading Water with the Arms above the Surface.
7. The Spinning Top.
8. Sculling on the Back with Head Foremost.
9. Sculling on the Back with Feet Foremost.

Membership in the third requires a successful examination in

10. Sculling on the Breast with the Head Foremost and Feet Foremost.
11. Porpoise Swimming.
12. The Steamboat.
13. Log-Rolling, Right and Left.
14. Undressing in the Water.

2. Reward for Special Excellence.

A medal or cup will be given each year to the student showing the best work in the requirements of the Honor Classes.

NECESSARY QUALIFICATIONS OF A TEACHER OF SWIMMING

A first class teacher of swimming should not only be familiar with the theory of the art, but should also be able to give a practical demonstration of every exercise contained in this manual. The swimming art once acquired is never forgotten. Great care, therefore, should be exercised in teaching the first lessons, lest the pupil acquire a faulty method. It is a well recognized fact that many self-taught swimmers fail to ever acquire the easy and graceful style so characteristic of those who have been well coached in theory and practice, and are, therefore, unable to swim long distances with ease and pleasure. A lack of knowledge among teachers in some other forms of physical education may do little harm, but in the art of swimming it is different, because life itself may depend upon a theoretical and practical knowledge of this, the most useful and beneficial of all physical exercises.

ERRATA

After " For long distance swimming " in the sixth line on page 29 add "in a rough sea," making the sentence read: " For long distance swimming in a rough sea this stroke is almost useless," etc.

In the second line on page 30 omit the word "scissors," making the first two lines read as follows: "advocates of the crawl stroke have already proven beyond doubt that the kick," etc.

In the twenty-eighth line on page 30 substitute the word "moderate" for "long," making the line read as follows: "A moderate Trudgen arm stroke combined with a," etc.

The last lines of the first paragraph on page 14 should read as follows: " The air should be drawn into the lungs when the arms are forced backward and expelled as they are thrust forward."

The third line of the last paragraph on page 15 should read as follows: "the palms turned outward, backward to the sides."

On page 19, the third line from the top should read: " The hands should be flat and the fingers together."